Reclaiming Sanity:
A Guidebook to Liberal Redemption

ISBN-13: 978-1725162044

Printed in the United States of America

Updated: 6/19

"If there is ever a fascist takeover in America, it will come not in the form of storm troopers kicking down doors but with lawyers and social workers saying. "I'm from the government and I'm here to help."
— Jonah Goldberg

"Never try to discourage thinking, for you are sure to succeed."
— Bertrand Russell

"I am just mystified by these people telling me I would think Obama was doing a great job if his skin contained less melanin."
— Jonah Goldberg

"Our tolerance is part of what makes Britain Britain. So conform to it, or don't come here."
— Tony Blair

"I need to say this — you shouldn't trust any government, actually including this one. You should not trust government — full stop. The natural inclination of government is to hoard power and information; to accrue power to itself in the name of the public good."
— Nick Clegg

"Liberalism is the ideology of Western suicide. When once this initial and final sentence is understood, everything about liberalism - the beliefs, emotions and values associated with it, the nature of its enchantment, its practical record, its future - falls into place."
— James Burnham

"The modern definition of a racist is someone who is winning an argument with a liberal."
— Peter Brimelow

Reclaiming Sanity:
A Guidebook to Liberal Redemption

By Lance Hodge

"Two things I've learned:

1) you simply cannot change someone's mind on certain issues and

2) some issues are so important you cannot stop trying to."

— J.S.B. Morse

Reclaiming Sanity:
A Guidebook to Liberal Redemption

By Lance Hodge

If you are a liberal, this book was most likely a gift. Somebody loves you, or at least cares about you. Between the covers of this little book lies the promise of *redemption*.

I won't be able to be nice here, sorry about that, that's probably a defect on my part, but this is an attempt at your redemption, sort of an intervention, and I think you need some straight talk, some brutal truths, to make the point here. Sometimes people need it in all caps, TO WAKE THEM UP! So I'll apologize ahead of time for the name-calling; it's a short book, bear with me.

You're probably a good person, but if you're a liberal you've made a critical mistake. You've bought into the flawed notion that "liberal" equals good and "conservative" equals bad. At first blush you may not believe you see it in those stark terms, but you probably do. *I* actually believe that, in reverse, that *liberals* are bad, and *conservatives* are good, in general, when it comes to political views. Mostly, this opinion is based on the simple presumption, that seems true based on their actions and proposals, that liberals are out to destroy this country and to turn it into something quite different than what our founders had in mind; and I think that's bad.

I won't fill this book with pro and con arguments, that's the stuff of FOX news vs. CNN, and competing arguments are often lost when the "news" is swallowed whole from the same bowl. But there is another bowl, the red pill or blue pill if you will, and the "sides" in this struggle are epic, and for the most part immutable. The hearts and minds of those on each side are not easily changed, and what is at stake is not simply competing political views or a harmless difference of opinion, what hangs in the balance is the continued existence of our Nation as founded.

The left has taken a hard turn, with many now *embracing* socialism, speaking openly of changing our Constitution, and becoming increasingly aggressive and confrontational against the concept of free speech. If someone shows up at a political protest wearing a Trump hat, for example, chances are good that the liberal mob will *forcibly* take that hat and are likely to be violent to its wearer. That is new, that is the new and radical left in the era of Trump, and why what we are witnessing lately is perhaps the stuff of massive civil unrest brewing, some say a potential civil war.

I've addressed this issue in other books, and there are probably a hundred ways to approach this; but at the heart of this debate is *diversity* and *tolerance*. If we divide all the people we know into their most general parts, politically, we generally end up with *liberals* and *conservatives*. There are always exceptions to the rule, but as a rule a liberal will not become a conservative and a conservative will not become a liberal, we are hard-wired, it is baked in. We believe what we believe and that's not easy to change. The *key* is to realize just *how* you arrived at those beliefs, and to be honest about how much you *really know* about the things you know.

That reality, that we won't usually change our social and political views makes this book, and others I've written to discuss such political subjects, largely useless. In the past we have mostly, on both sides, been *tolerant* of our divergent views, but lately tolerance has given way to brutish tactics to *silence* the opposition. The *left* is *intolerant* and unable to coexist peaceably with a diverse (different) viewpoint, especially when Donald Trump is the key factor in those differences. TDS, *Trump Derangement Syndrome* is real; the left is truly deranged and out of control. If you don't believe that, keep reading.

Our hard-wired differences are most likely unchangeable, due mostly to a biased media onslaught out to manipulate the news and create an *alternate reality* that feeds and incites the left. When facts are dismissed and our political views play only to *emotion*, we are in dangerous territory. Although this book, and its effort at redemption, is likely to fail, I like to think that it's worth the effort, if only a few hearts and minds are changed, so, I'll try.

Redemption will not be for the masses, it will come one by one, as some liberals see the light, perhaps as the left's embrace of socialism and the attack on our Constitution becomes too much to take, and as the left's violence and intolerance betrays their radical anti-America agenda, and as good people realize that the *fake news* media is indeed an arm of one political party, not a fair and free independent press. That term, "Fake news" has been earned.

Again, if you're a liberal this book was most likely a gift. A liberal wouldn't buy a book that seeks to point out how wrong they are in hopes of changing them, and most liberals will not sit through this onslaught of the truth.

On that subject of *change*, and our desire to convince the other side that they are wrong; that is the key to understanding the largely impossible task of converting political viewpoints, and, as a bonus, is the key to understanding many failures in *marriage*. Especially with women, they believe they can change the man. But he doesn't change, or he resents changing, and in either case he resents the woman for trying to change him, and the marriage fails. A leopard can't change his spots. Like I said, *"...as a rule a liberal will not become a conservative and a conservative will not become a liberal, we are hard-wired, it is baked in."*

For this reason, this book will be short, more a pamphlet than a book, because I don't want to waste your time or mine.

The title of this book says a lot. ***Reclaiming Sanity: A Guidebook to Liberal Redemption.***

Liberals allow themselves to adopt some level of *insanity*, increasingly on display as of the writing of this book.

This is from *Mirriam-Webster*:

<u>**INSANITY**</u>

: a **severely disordered state of the mind**

: **unsoundness of mind or lack of the ability to
understand**

: **extreme folly or unreasonableness**
the *insanity* of violence

And <u>***redemption***</u>:

: serving **to offset or compensate for a defect**

Well that's not nice, I guess, and is part of the
reason this book had to arrive as a gift, this stuff is pretty
insulting, it seems.

Although I just can't help myself as far as insults go
when discussing the wildly *wrong* thinking of the left, the
goal here is *understanding* not to insult. You will need
introspection here, and, so you don't *too* feel picked on,
we'll do the same review of a conservative view shortly.

Before we get more specific, you should accept
yourself as part of a "team." You're either on the *liberal*
team or the *conservative* team, for the most part. It's very
informative, and enlightening, to look at the general
behavior of your team when it comes to political debate. I
vote *republican*, but I can't stand them! If there were
another viable party, with a clear *Tea Party* agenda, I'd
vote for *that* party. So rather than frame this in terms of

democrat or republican, *liberal* and *conservative* is more descriptive.

Let's take a few simple, general examples.

Protests. Liberals like to protest more than conservatives do. But from time to time conservatives do protest. Pick a couple of high-profile protests, two organized by and populated with conservatives and two organized by and populated with liberals. You might have to Google this if you don't watch much news, or if you only pay attention to one type of news, liberal or conservative. I'll give you one example, the protests about civil war monuments. The typical conservative protest was largely non-violent and non-aggressive, while the typical liberal protest on this matter was quite aggressive, violent, and destructive (tearing down statues.) You may not know this, but that's the *norm*, conservatives generally do not fight with people, burn things, destroy property, threaten violence, or attempt to shut down and silence those with an opposing view. In contrast, liberal protests are more often than not quite aggressive, often violent, and more likely to become destructive; and those liberal protestors often do seek to silence those with another point of view, to shout in their face with bull horns, to shut down the differing view, to disallow rational debate. You know which group feels the need to wear masks and to hide their identity while they protest, it's those violent liberals. I know which team I think represents the most reasonable way to dissent in this society, and it's not the liberal team. If you're a liberal, that ought to bother you, being on that team; that's a *big* thing.

Do you think violence and shutting down the other point of view is right? It isn't.

Another example. This will date this book a bit, but Donald Trump will most likely be reelected so we have a few years. Make a list, **why** do you so *hate* Donald Trump?

1.

2.

3.

4.

5.

Did you have five reasons? Was one of them how disgusting Donald Trump was to talk about grabbing women's *ussies? (Look at me, self-censoring.) If you forgot that one you can go back and add it. Do you recall what that quote was about? It was in 2005, you know he didn't run for President until 2016, right? That remark was talking about what some women will let you do if you're a star, if you're rich and famous. Basically he was saying some women will be very submissive and very slutty in the presence of stardom and money. Do you think that's incorrect? It's a reflection of a reality that most of the rich and famous would quickly confirm; and those of you with just a *little* common sense and street smarts must know this to be true. THAT'S why you hate Donald Trump? I hope you also hate most other rich and famous men, to be consistent. This "Trump hates women" mantra is ridiculous and doesn't hold up in the face of facts. I think it's quite clear that Donald Trump, and most men, LOVE women.

I wonder what's on the rest of your list. Because he's a *racist*? I imagine you have some proof of that? Actually, I imagine you don't. Just recently Trump was *confirmed* to be a racist because he said, or implied, that several people weren't very bright. Some of those people were black, so *of course* he's a racist. But he's said the same thing about plenty of white people, what about that? And, to be fair, the black people he said weren't very bright, well, they are well known to say some pretty stupid things. It seems that liberals will jump to label as *racist* <u>any</u> remark made by Trump about a non-white person. Again, *not* racist, to point out that someone's comments are stupid. *(Of course stupid is in the eye of the beholder, but when it comes to Maxine Waters for example, that level of stupid goes way beyond any skin color, she's just plain stupid, in any color.)*

Was one of your reasons to hate the President because he wants a border wall? He *must* hate Mexicans. And because he wants to keep America-hating Muslims out of the country, he obviously hates Muslims. Really? You have a problem with those things? You think having an open border is a good thing? It isn't. You think allowing people, whoever they are, into our country when those people *hate* this country is a good idea? It isn't. I don't want to call liberals stupid, but *really*. Every nation has strong immigration laws, have you tried moving to Canada, or even Mexico? Good luck, they'll only let you in if you're rich or have some very critical skill they need. A strong physical border barrier is also important to slow down the massive influx of drugs into the country. Wanting a strong border and a border wall is just common sense, it's surprising that you don't realize that.

Did your list have "He hates LGTBQ's?" I think I left out a letter or two. Actually, Trump is pretty liberal there. Did you know that Hillary Clinton and Barack Obama thought marriage should be strictly between a man and a woman, before changing that view for political reasons? You knew that? I'll bet you didn't.

I'm not psychic, but your list *must* be filled with baseless *emotion*, not *facts*. The *facts* don't support such anti-Trump vitriol.

Because you liberals base your "resistance" of Trump largely on *emotion* not fact, you would find it hard to debate this topic with a conservative, you would most likely depend on that emotion, then find that you have no facts to support your hate, and would quickly find your side of the argument is pretty weak. I'll bet such a debate would end up with you angry and abruptly ending that discussion, perhaps with some choice curse words, or some parting charge of racism.

If you had *facts*, they should have ended up on that list you made. Did they? If you notice your list is made up of *emotional arguments*, not facts, you might begin to see you have a problem with *critical thinking*, but, if you're lucky, you aren't beyond redemption.

Because the goal here is *redemption*, you'll have to work with me a bit. You'll have to set aside some of that indoctrination from that liberal media and step out of the "Resist Trump" mindset for a few moments.

P.S. *In case you don't know it, the* <u>liberal media</u> *is really MOST media:*

MSNBC
CNN
ABC
NBC
CBS
Google
Twitter
Facebook
And the list goes on…

As of the writing of this book Donald Trump has been President for about two years. You liberals don't know it, but he's been *wildly* successful. The economy is experiencing levels of growth that Obama deemed impossible. Obama thought, and said, that Trump would need "a magic wand" to improve the economy in the ways that Trump has achieved. It seems all that all Trump needed was a strong belief in the inherent greatness of America and good strategies to promote and grow business. It worked, the economy is booming, manufacturing jobs are returning to the U.S. with major businesses spending billions on new plants, for the first time the U.S. has become the world's largest oil producer, unemployment in all sectors is at all-time *record* low rates (especially black, Hispanic, and women) and just recently Trump's strategy on correcting our trade imbalances with other countries is beginning to result in more equitable trade and larger profits for American producers. Trump's firm stance on NATO has resulted in other countries paying BILLIONS more of their fair share to NATO. Trump is doing what he promised during the election and succeeding. If you only listened to CNN or the news feed on your social media, you might not know any of this. The liberal media's reporting on Trump is consistently around 90% negative, although Trump's popularity in polls is over 50% and is higher than Obama's approval level at this point in his presidency! The term "fake news" is accurate, they don't even *try* to report on the positive aspects of this Presidency, the liberal media is part of the Trump *resistance*, and they demonstrate that daily. A clearly biased media should worry you, our Nation cannot long survive without a free and fair press. When our "journalists" lose their independence, they are likely to become a tool of government, or a tool of one political party, which is what has happened now with virtually all media against republicans and in support of democrats. A media on the side of one political party and willing to manipulate the "news" to serve them, ultimately leads to tyranny and oppression.

Just recently a purge has begun on social media; with the cover and excuse of deleting "Hate speech" and bringing about "Fairness." Social media giants have begun purging, deleting, conservative thought and opinion. These are dangerous times when our ability to speak freely and to have opposing views is disallowed. The first amendment of our Constitution enshrined our right to speak freely, and it is that speech you *most* <u>disagree</u> with that is most in need of protection. We learn by listening to other views.

You'll have to accept some facts, for this redemption to work. The points made above are true. President Trump is doing a good job. The economy is thriving, businesses are expanding, manufacturing is returning to the U.S., taxes have been reduced, thousands of redundant or overly oppressive federal regulations have been removed, there are millions less in need of food stamps, and America is becoming greater by the day. You liberals will cringe at all that, thinking it's all lies, but it's all true. Your liberal media is not reporting the facts, they focus on misguided negative *emotion*, as part of the anti-Trump resistance. A free and fair press is missing in action.

Your top five reasons for hating Trump should have turned on a light for you. You should see that you've fallen for some BS, you've been a pawn of that fake news media, and you're much like a lemming, marching in line with the crowd, oblivious to much, and if the lemming in charge walks off a cliff, all the other lemmings follow. That's not a good strategy, you should be eager to seek out *facts*, not to rely on rhetoric and emotion, and to use your *critical thinking skills* to find the truth. It is happening, even Kanye West, and an increasing number of blacks, have seen the light when it comes to Donald Trump, and are supporting him, and are thinking for themselves not as a group, which is the hallmark of *critical thinking*.

I mentioned earlier that this same test of *fact vs. emotion* should be applied to conservatives. During his campaign Donald Trump made many promises, and unlike most politicians, he's keeping those promises. I'll use myself as an example here. I'll list five reasons why I *support* President Trump, in no particular order.

1. He's putting America first when it comes to **trade**. That's new. For a long time politicians have played political games with trade polices with other nations, most often to the disadvantage of the U.S. Trump is out to correct our long-standing trade imbalances, making trade with other nations more equitable, and more profitable for the U.S. That's important.

2. He's out to tighten up our lax and unfair **border/immigration laws**. Immigrants by the many millions would love to flood into the United States in search of a better life. It's true that many countries around the world are "shit holes." Listen to the immigrants from many of these countries, their stories of suffering make it clear that that term is often quite descriptive. If we have unrestricted or massive immigration we will be overrun with unskilled workers who will cost us more than they will contribute. No country can survive an unlimited welfare economy. A wall makes sense, strong immigration policies make sense, and taking in immigrants that can make a positive contribution and fewer who will not, makes sense. You don't have to hate anyone to realize such polices are simply a reflection of economic realities.

3. He's reducing overly burdensome **government regulations** that unnecessarily hinder the growth of business. Our Constitution mandated a *limited* federal government, not a massive leviathan intruding on every aspect of life. The Trump administration has cut more of those burdensome and unnecessary regulations than ever before, and business is growing because of it. That's a good thing.

4. He's **reduced taxes**. Trump enacted the biggest tax cut in history. *The People* got more money in their paychecks, business had more money to invest and hire, and ***after* that tax cut the federal government collected record revenues!** As of the writing of this book the U.S. economy is thriving, breaking records for growth, and far surpassing Trump's predicted levels of economic growth. Unemployment is at all-time lows for all, especially for blacks, Hispanics, and women. His economic policies are working.

5. Donald Trump is a businessman, he's used to **solving problems to make things work,** and to make a business profitable. Applying such principles to the American economy is new, even republicans are fighting the President as he tries to change the way things have been done in our ineffective and out of control government for many decades. Trump's policies are working to improve our economy and the lives of the people.

There's more to talk about; the environment, oil, global warming, the supreme court, abortion, etc. The left, *liberals*, would have you believe that Trump's views on such things, or on *everything*, is wrong, and destructive, and out to destroy the world. They call him a Nazi, a racist, homophobic, a misogynist, etc. To you liberals reading this, you probably welcomed those reminders, as you shook your head in agreement, yes! Nazi, racist, homophobe, woman hater, etc. Yes! Again, you've got facts, right? Just how is the President *any* of those things? *Facts*, not some *emotional* argument. You'll find such facts hard to come by, unless you've simply replaced *emotion* with facts, since most liberals seem quite content to *dismiss* facts, and proof, in place of some emotional argument that might sound great shouted from a megaphone as the crowd chants "Impeach Trump."

Again, I won't try to do a point counterpoint to every topic I can think of, I think we can make the point generally that the liberal media is *editing* your news, and *shaping* it in favor of the left and to the detriment of the President. One specific point, that might be resolved soon, is this *Russia* thing.

You liberals; do you actually think Donald Trump is a Russian spy? Conspiring with Russia to the detriment of the U.S.? Really? Really? Do you think, despite proof this did not happen, that Trump joined forces with Putin to fix the Presidential election, because Russia would much rather have a President Trump than a President Hillary? Really? When the facts all come out, and most likely it becomes clear that this whole Russia thing was completely democratic B.S., will you liberals finally admit that the "Lemming" analogy fits? You should.

(<u>Update</u>: The Mueller report came out and Trump was NOT a Russian spy, and after more than two years and tens of millions of dollars spent, a team of Trump-hating lawyers couldn't find ANYTHING to charge Donald Trump with.)

You've been played by your liberal media, and you went right along with it, willingly, tossing common sense out the window. As for "collusion" with the Russians, your liberal media has most likely hidden this from you, but it is clear as more evidence is exposed, that those colluding with Russia were *democrats*, especially Hillary Clinton!

When a conservative debates a liberal there should be something made clear at the onset. Ask the liberal this question before wasting too much time debating them (you liberals reading this, if you're old enough, ask yourselves.) During the eight years of Obama, can you list the TERRIBLE things Obama and his administration did? Is there *anything* on your list? How many things? Did you come up with five? Does your list include any of this?

Benghazi, the ***Fast and Furious*** gun running scandal, billions in **cash paid to Iran**, the ridiculous **Iran Nuclear Deal**, failed **Obamacare** and Obamacare lies, **Hillary Clinton's Russia dealings for our uranium**, the many millions of dollars from Russia to Bill and **Hillary's "foundation,"** Obama whispering to the Russians that he "could be more flexible after the election," **Obama's hidden college records, Obama's friendship with an American terrorist**, Obama's being **raised as a Muslim** in Indonesia, Obama saying the Islamic call to prayer was the most beautiful sound in the world, **Obama's communist mentor** during his youth, Obama's opinion that manufacturing jobs lost to other countries would never come back, that the U.S. needed to get used to low economic growth and performance, and that Trump would need a "magic wand" to improve it, the **IRS targeting of Tea Party groups, Obama's repeated attacks on the police, Obama's attacks on the Second Amendment** and his distain for our Constitution, **Obama's Attorney General being held in contempt of Congress**, Obama's *massive* increase in federal spending and our National Debt… to name a few.

So ask a *conservative* why they don't like, or perhaps *hate*, some politician, and you'll most likely get some *facts*, not *emotional rhetoric*. If you didn't have much of a negative list for Obama, you are just where *they* want you, brainwashed by your liberal media who hid or minimized much of the above to prop up Obama. And, if you were old enough during the Obama years and didn't have anything negative to say about Obama, you really disqualify yourself from commenting on current politics, because you simply don't pay much attention; you aren't much of a critical thinker; you accept your liberal news sources as factual, and *emotion* is probably all you have for your side of the argument; you seem OK pushing aside *facts*. This is one reason why the liberal left would rather shout down and shut down the other side, knowing they don't have the facts to support their supposed outrage.

Yikes! This is some gift! If a friend or family member gave you this book, I hope that relationship survives. This is pretty brutal, but I'm trying to save you! Hang in there…

Another example, since you probably need more convincing, is the *outrage* (by liberals) over children being separated from their parents at the border. Oh-my-God! Can you believe it! What sort of people would rip a child away from their parent! Nazis! Evil Trump, heartless conservatives, that's who!

Before I continue, can you think of ANY reason why children would be separated from their parents when caught illegally entering the country? *Any* reasons? The liberal media doesn't talk about *reasons*, they seem to think that separating children from their parents at the border is unthinkable, terrible, evil, criminal… that's what you think right?

This is a *universal* theme among liberals; I don't think you're *really* a liberal if you don't buy into this "child separation" outrage, it's **so** clear to liberals, and to all the mainstream media, and to all of social media, and to every late night TV show host, that this is simply and clearly and so obviously wrong, and cannot be defended. How do you defend ripping a child away from their parents? How? This is clear proof (if you want **facts**) that Trump is evil, conservatives are evil, and they're racists! There you go, there's your FACTS!

That *critical thinking* I was talking about, or a lack of it in this case, has a lot to do with a *defective prefrontal cortex*, and actual *damage* (defects in the 'wiring' of a liberal's brain, effecting their ability to employ critical thinking regarding some subjects.) I'll discuss that prefrontal cortex problem in a little more detail before we're done. But right now, if you *can* use some critical thinking about this subject, you'll discover this.

a. Crossing our border illegally is, *illegal*.

b. When you commit a crime (something illegal) you are sometimes *arrested*.

c. When you're arrested, and you end up detained or in jail, and if you have a child with you, your child doesn't stay with you in jail. They don't serve your sentence with you, they don't go to court with you. The child is taken away (Oh the humanity!) and given to relatives or put in foster care. That's how it works, that's how it *always* works when you commit a crime. Rob a bank, with your child in your arms, and get arrested; what will happen to that child? They'll serve 2 to 10 in the federal penitentiary with you? No, they'll be taken from you. Duh. THAT'S why the children are taken away with these border arrests, the parents are working their way through our criminal justice system. Along with other reasons such as, sometimes the adult with the child isn't even the parent, they are a sex trafficker, kidnapper, a rapist, etc. (DNA testing is done on all these kids to determine this.) Put just a *little* critical thinking into this "children separated at the border" situation and you ought to lose some of that outrage, as you begin to THINK.

P.S. If you looked up the numbers of children separated from parents at the border during the Obama years, you'd find some HUGE numbers, and of course you and your liberal media were outraged then, right? Or, is this <u>suddenly</u> an earth-shaking issue, when Trump became President? Again, you're being manipulated by a media that finds you pretty easy to manipulate; and that should anger you. Note: I'm not sure that they're still using them, but some detained children were kept in CAGES (basically chain-link fencing) and those CAGES were constructed during the Obama Presidency!

At some point, if this book is working, you should have some lights come on, you might have an *epiphany!* You might wake up to the fact that you've been played, and that conservatives *aren't* evil, don't hate women, don't want to destroy the earth, aren't racists, etc. If this book is working, your world has just become very complicated. Now what? What about all your crazy liberal friends?

You've been wearing that team jersey for a long time, maybe all your adult life, and that's a tough move to make, switching teams, or even beginning to *question* the motives and tactics of your team; you might lose some of those friends. Think about poor Kanye West, (who has voiced support of Donald Trump) in his massive circle of liberal friends and family, they must not talk politics, or he's lost some friends.

But, not to worry, as I said at the outset, a liberal is not likely to suddenly become a conservative, and a conservative is *certainly* unlikely to become a liberal, so all is well, the status quo will remain intact, and both our sides can continue this war.

Speaking of war, there is increasing talk of *civil war* in this country, and as liberals escalate their violent protests, and continue their physical attacks on conservatives, it certainly has that potential. The thing about the liberal side of this "war" is their willingness to believe that America and Capitalism is the problem. They even think that old dusty Constitution of ours is the problem, just as Barack Obama was on a mission to "transform" this country into some *other* country. If democrats don't rein in their "resist" rhetoric and denounce the increasingly violent actions of their liberal followers, this potential war could become real.

The recent liberal embrace of socialism is at odds with the existence of America. Our Constitution isn't compatible with socialism; our founders realized the historic failures and resulting tyranny and suffering of socialism and soundly rejected that system as they built our Constitutional Republic. The current liberal trend is to continue Obama's *transformation* of the United States into some other country; and that my friends *is* the stuff of a civil war.

Let's see, we're almost done here. This little book will be about thirty pages or so, making it a quick read. For the conservative, it will save you some time and frustration, making these points yourself. Just give your liberal friend or family member this book and see what happens. Often, we simply don't engage those friends and family in such conversations, when we know it will be confrontational; so I've done the confronting for you. You're welcome.

For you liberals who actually sat down and took a few minutes to read this, congratulations, you're the exception to the rule. I hope this little exercise opened a window, turned on a light, knocked off those rose-colored glasses for a few minutes, and got you thinking *differently* about this *liberal vs. conservative* struggle.

The "fake news" label is accurate. Liberal media is jaded, they have clearly taken sides, and they will not report accurately when it comes to President Trump. As I mentioned earlier, I *despise* the democrat AND republican parties as a whole. These professional politicians are dedicated *first* to politics, with the interests of *The People* coming in a distant second. It's quite informative to listen to some FOX news, then to some CNN. I do that a lot, and it's eye-opening. Although FOX tilts obviously conservative, they do a better job than CNN at reporting the opposing view. The biggest problem with CNN and with other liberal media (social media) is the clear *withholding* of some news. They *shape* their news with the one-sided reporting, lack of facts, and constant editorializing rather than simply reporting; that has prompted Trump's "fake news" mantra.

Several pages back I mentioned the ***prefrontal cortex,*** and the fact that some liberals may have some *damage* to that part of their brain, making it hard, maybe impossible to do the critical thinking needed to accept the premise of this book, and the points I've made here. This prefrontal cortex explanation makes clear for the first time how liberals can be so blind to common sense and facts. The inability of liberals to grasp *facts* has long perplexed conservatives. What seems *crazy* thinking to conservatives might have an explanation, a defective prefrontal cortex!

The following is from a book I wrote, ***The Book of HATE***, which covers in more detail many of these *conservative vs. liberal* issues. This is not my opinion; it comes from established research on the brain. Here's what I said about that prefrontal cortex problem.

THE LIBERAL BRAIN:

It's clear to conservatives that liberals must be crazy. Turns out that isn't far from the truth, there does seem to be a defect in the liberal brain involving the prefrontal cortex.

This information from *Wikipedia* on the following pages discusses the **results of adult damage to various parts of the brain and frontal cortex,** and *the decision-making results of such brain damage.*

It is logical to see these specific examples as a window into understanding such brain *defects* in a more general sense.

Our brains are not mature until we are about **25 years old,** it is during these formative years that a failure to 'use' *critical thinking* may doom us to live with a miswired brain, a brain incapable of proper logical and fact-based analysis on *some* subjects, which may last a lifetime. Science seems to believe that this defect may explain the twisted and illogical nature of *liberal thinking*.

We don't necessarily have to undergo *physical* trauma to the brain to *damage* it. The early development of our brain, and the later adolescent and young adult maturing process of the prefrontal cortex, can result in similar *damage*. As we mature, the brain naturally **prunes away** little-used connections. If we are not raised as *critical thinkers*, and <u>practice</u> *informed reasoning* while we are young (before age 25) we may lose those abilities in some areas, permanently. If neuro connections are missing, or miswired during this maturation period, the result is a less than optimal functioning portion of the brain, ***with similar defects in logic, emotion, and decision-making as might be experienced with physical trauma to the brain.***

This revelation may provide the missing link to understanding the strange and contradictory behaviors of the liberal mind in some areas, and specifically in some *subjects*, in the presence of an otherwise functional and even otherwise highly intelligent and logical individuals. Remember, if you spend your formative years in an environment where both sides of issues are *not* examined, where some liberal professor, some media, or your peer group 'tells you what to think' and you simply adopt that view, well, you haven't thought it out, you haven't used all those neuropathways that let you *reason*, to think *critically*, and ultimately those little used pathways are pruned away, and you are left with a brain *incapable* of such reasoned evaluation of differing views in certain areas, **a defective prefrontal cortex.**

This list details some specific areas of thinking and reasoning defects when *damage to the prefrontal cortex has occurred.* Some bells should ring here, look in the mirror, or at the reflection of someone close to you…

Do these signs of a malfunctioning prefrontal cortex seem familiar to you?

Do they mirror the behavior of the liberal mind?

Impaired **moral judgment**

Severe impairments in personal and social **decision-making**

Impaired capacity to learn from their mistakes, *making the same decisions again and again even though they lead to negative consequences*

*Seem to be **blind to the future consequences of their actions***

*More **easily influenced** by misleading advertising*

*There is a gap in reasoning when applying the same moral principles to similar situations in their own lives. The result is that people make **decisions that are inconsistent with their self-professed moral values***

*More likely to endorse **self-serving actions that break moral rules or cause harm to others***

*Causes **failure in using correct moral emotion***

*Causes impairments of **behavioral control and decision making***

***Impulsive** murderers (and those prone to violence) have decreased activity in the prefrontal cortex*

*Lower activation in the prefrontal cortex is also correlated with **antisocial behavior***

Show defects both in **emotional response and emotion regulation**

They show markedly **reduced social emotions such as compassion, shame and guilt.** *These are emotions that are closely associated with moral values. Patients also exhibit* **poorly regulated anger and frustration tolerance** *in certain circumstances*

Changes such as **lack of empathy, irresponsibility, and poor decision making.** *These traits are similar to psychopathic personality traits*

That's something to think about…

If we look at a political demonstration by liberals, we often see extreme anger issues on display, lack of tolerance, lack of control, lack of empathy as they burn and destroy the property of others, poor decision making, irresponsible and illegal behavior, even physical assaults on those they disagree with, and a seeming disregard for the consequences of their actions. Those protestors often wear masks, looking much like the terrorists who practice similar tactics. We see many of those signs we just discussed, that indicate pre-frontal cortex brain issues. And, interestingly, at a political demonstration put on by conservatives, we see little or none of that. It is the interaction with liberal protestors with

such prefontal cortex problems where these
issues arise. Interesting.

There we go. Hopefully this little book will change some hearts and minds. I hope redemption is yours, and from now on you break free of ANY group-think, liberal *or* conservative, and think for *yourself*, based on common sense and *factual* evidence.

Note*: There's a chance that you might be able to repair some of that miswired brain by employing critical thinking skills on controversial topics, especially if you're still young, it may not be hopeless, you might still chart that path to redemption!*

The End

P.S. *If you don't know, liberal thinking is the norm in education. You were more-than-likely raised in an educational environment populated by leftist liberals. They have an agenda, and they made sure you were immersed in their way of thinking. If you didn't know that, now you do, and you can break free. Don't form your opinions and beliefs based on some groupthink, make sure YOU <u>think</u> about it, and decide where <u>your</u> beliefs and <u>your</u> moral compass lies, based on knowledge, not indoctrination.*

"I began to realize that maybe my opinions just didn't fit in with the liberal status quo, which seems to mean that you must absolutely hate Trump, his supporters and everything they believe. If you dare not to protest or boycott Trump, you are a traitor.
If you dare to question liberal stances or make an effort toward understanding why conservatives think the way they do, you are a traitor. It can seem like liberals are actually against free speech if it fails to conform with the way they think. And I don't want to be a part of that club anymore."

— Chadwick Moore

"The U.S. didn't achieve its liberty or prosperity by mistake. It was by design, and the architects were the Founding Fathers. Don't mess with the Constitution. The Constitution matters."

— A.E. Samaan

Other books by **Lance Hodge** are available at **Amazon.com**, Barnes & Noble, Books A Million, and fine booksellers everywhere